THE PRACTICE OF THE PRESENCE OF GOD

In Modern English

BROTHER LAWRENCE

Translated by Jessica Turner and Amy Catchpole

Title: *The Practice of the Presence of God (In Modern English)*
Author: Brother Lawrence
Modern English Translation: Jessica Turner & Amy Catchpole

ISBN: 978-1-7645853-3-0

Published by Olivet Publishing Pty Ltd

Imprint: Olivet Classics

TABLE OF CONTENTS

PREFACE

This short but powerful piece of classic Christian literature, gifted to the world during the 17th Century, contains the collected teachings of Brother Lawrence (born Nicolas Herman), a humble and devout lover of God.

This book is one that has profoundly impacted the lives of many, including my own. And still, to this day, many years since I first picked it up, the wisdom and spiritual principles contained in this book help to guide my own life. There have been moments when I've been caught up in mundane tasks, and reminded that there's a gift within every moment; not just those that have a spiritual appearance which allows us to become aware of the presence of God. This is because He dwells within us in the same way during our washing of dishes, as He does when we are in a place of prayer. Practicing the presence of God is a principle for life that is truly transformational.

I embarked on the quest to translate this beautiful piece of writing into one that modern readers, centuries later, can enjoy without the barriers that arise from reading the original text in its early English format. I have taken care to ensure that no meaning or intent from the original author is lost in translation, and that the full weight of the text is preserved.

ABOUT BROTHER LAWRENCE

Brother Lawrence, also known as Brother Lawrence of the Resurrection, was born in 1611, in the town of Hériménil, which is located in modern-day eastern France. Born to peasants during the Thirty Years' War, Herman was no stranger to poverty. With limited schooling and few opportunities, he joined the army, which would guarantee daily meals and a modest stipend. As a teenager serving in the army, Herman began to experience the beginnings of a powerful spiritual journey. In his writings, Brother Lawrence recounts the experience that first began his incredible move towards spirituality – he came across a lifeless tree amidst a battlefield. Despite the tree appearing dead and forlorn, he came to the realization that by springtime, this tree would be transformed into a glorious spectacle of leaf and flower. With that comprehension came the revelation that God, too, can transform the human heart in much the same way. Seeing the 'providence and power of God' hidden within the tree, Nicholas Herman had been stirred from deep within, unto the presence of God.

Continuing in his army service, Herman witnessed many horrors of war, which were burnt into his mind forever, although he spoke little of these experiences. After being injured on duty, and rendered permanently lame, he retired from his post, and after going back to his religious roots during a period of solitude, he took a job as a footman for William de Fuibert, treasurer to the king of France. He described himself during the period of this role, as "a great, awkward fellow who broke everything."

After his service as a footman, Nicholas heeded an inner call to follow in the footsteps of his uncle, a holy Discalced Carmelite. In June of 1640, he joined the Discalced Carmelite Priory; a monastery in Paris, where the rest of his life was to be spent. With this new life path came a new identity, as Nicholas Herman then became known as Brother Lawrence of the Resurrection. He entered the monastery as a lay brother, and his role from that point on was to work in the kitchen, and later, to repair sandals. Most would not deem these duties 'holy', at first glance, but when you peer closer at the way

Brother Lawrence approached these tedious tasks, what you will see is profoundly holy, indeed.

Brother Lawrence, in the midst of cooking and washing dishes, developed a set of rules for a holy life, which came to be known as 'practicing the presence of God' – the practice of turning the inward affections of the heart towards the Lord, at every moment of every day. He based his life on this simple yet powerful practice, and began to walk in unprecedented levels of peace, attracting many visitors who sought his spiritual guidance and wisdom. Brother Lawrence went home to be with the Lord on 12 February, 1691, unaware that his humble life would leave a rich spiritual legacy, that would be savored by young and old, for centuries to come. Two years after his passing, 'The Practice of the Presence of God' was first published.

This book contains the notes from conversations, as well as letters, exchanged between Brother Lawrence and Abbot Father Joseph de Beaufort. This translation also includes the Spiritual Maxims that were found in the room of Brother Lawrence after his death, and which were then published, along with the conversations and letters, by de Beaufort, under the title, 'Spiritual Maxims'.

I trust that you, like Brother Lawrence, would be taken deeper into the awareness of the presence of God surrounding you, even in the midst of the busyness, distraction, and duty that life brings.

"There doesn't exist in the world a life more sweet and delightful than that of a continual conversation with God." – Brother Lawrence

CONVERSATIONS

The first time I saw Brother Lawrence was on the 3rd of August, 1666. He told me that God had done him a remarkable favor by more deeply awakening his faith at the age of 18.

He said that seeing a tree lose its leaves in winter, and knowing that very soon the leaves would start to grow back, and that shortly after that, the flowers and fruit would start to appear, he was able to clearly see the providence and power of God. Ever since that time, nothing has been able to remove that knowledge from his soul. He said that this impression had set him free from the world, and started such a burning love for God in him, that he couldn't say whether it had ever increased in the forty years since that time.

Brother Lawrence told me that before becoming a monk, he had been a footman in the service of the treasurer,

Monsieur Fieubert. He described himself as a big, clumsy man who broke everything.

He said he had wanted to be accepted into a monastery, believing that he would there be punished for his clumsiness and mistakes. In this way, he hoped to sacrifice his life and all its pleasures to God, but he was disappointed in this, because all he found at the monastery was satisfaction.

He said that we should keep ourselves connected to God, always feeling His presence through regular prayer, as if in a continual conversation, and that it is shameful to stop talking to God simply to think about silly and minor things.

He said we should feed and nourish our souls by continually thinking about God, which would bring us great, overflowing joy from our devotion to Him.

Brother Lawrence advised that we should intensify our faith, and let it flourish. He said that it was a pity we had so little to begin with, and that, instead of basing their actions on their faith, men allowed their devotion to wander between varying beliefs, regularly changing their minds. He said that faith was the spirit of the Church, and that it was enough to bring us to perfection.

He said that we should give both our physical and spiritual selves up to God, and find contentment only in serving Him. It shouldn't matter whether He leads us through times of suffering or comfort, because there is no real difference to a soul completely given to the service of God. He said that we must be faithful during the difficult times, when we feel distant from God, and prayer feels like a struggle. During these times, God is testing our love for Him, and this is when we should even more deeply resign ourselves to Him, as this will aid us in our spiritual advancement.

Brother Lawrence said that he was completely unsurprised by the world's unhappiness and sin, which he heard of on a daily basis. He was, in fact, surprised that there was not more, knowing the wickedness sinners were capable of. He prayed for these sinners, but knowing that God could remedy their wrongs if He wanted, Brother Lawrence left it in the hands of God, and didn't concern himself with it any longer.

He said that to give ourselves over entirely to God, as He requires, we should be aware of all the worldly passions that live inside us, alongside our spiritual desires, and that God would give us awareness of those passions if we were truly devoted to Him. Brother Lawrence said that if I was sincere in wanting to serve God, I could come and see him whenever I wished, and I wouldn't be a nuisance to him, but if I was not completely devoted, I should not visit him again.

Second Conversation

Brother Lawrence said that he had always been driven by unselfish love, and that having resolved to make God's love the purpose of all his actions, he felt that this was the best method. He was pleased when he could complete any action for the love of God, no matter how small, and he wanted nothing more than God, not even the gifts He could bestow.

He said he had been concerned, for a time, with the belief that he was damned, and that nobody could convince him otherwise. But he had comforted himself with the knowledge that he engaged in a religious life, only for the love of God, and that he tried to take every action only for His glory. Whether damned or not, he would always choose to act purely for the love of God. He would die knowing that he had done everything he could to love Him.

He had struggled with this belief for four years, and during that time, endured much suffering. But he had eventually realized that his fear of damnation had come from a lack of faith, and once he had come to terms with that, his life began to pass in continual freedom and happiness. He had given his sins to God to show Him that he did not deserve God's favors, but God continued to bless him in abundance.

In order to create the habit of praying to God regularly, and offering to Him all our actions, Brother Lawrence said we must start off very diligently, but that after a while, we will find it easy to be called to prayer by God's love.

After all the pleasant days he had been given by God, he had expected his share of pain and suffering, but he was not worried about it, because he could do nothing to prevent it, and he knew that God would give him the strength to bear it.

Whenever he asked God to assist him in completing some virtuous act, saying, "Lord, I cannot do this unless You empower me", he always received more than enough strength to complete the task.

If ever he failed to do what he intended, he confessed his faults to God, saying, "I will always fail if You leave me alone, only You can hold me up and fix whatever is wrong". After giving his worries to God, he felt no more concern for the problem.

He said that we should endeavor to speak simply and plainly with God, only begging for assistance with our problems as they arose. God would never fail to grant His assistance, as Brother Lawrence had experienced many times.

He told of how he had recently been sent into Burgundy to buy wine for the monastery; a task he didn't enjoy, because he wasn't business-minded, and he was disabled, so he could only move around the boat by rolling himself over the casks. He didn't let his disability or the buying of the wine bother him, though. He told God that he was doing this for Him, and afterwards found he was able to do the job quite well. The year before, he had been sent into Auvergne for the same reason, and he said he couldn't give details of the event, but that it had also gone very well.

Brother Lawrence was also not at all fond of working in the kitchens, but he focused on doing all his work there for the love of God, and with regular prayers, asking God for the grace to do his job well, he found the work quite easy during his 15 years of service.

He said that he was very happy in his current post, but that he was as willing to leave it as he had been the previous job, because he was always happy, no matter where he was, when he was completing small acts for the love of God.

He said that he didn't think of set times of prayer as being different to any other time. He would take his prayer times, as directed by his superiors, but he did not need, or ask for, time off from work to pray, because no job, no matter how big, would keep him away from God.

Brother Lawrence told me that because he knew full well his obligation to love God in all things, and because that was his intention, he didn't feel the need for a director to advise him in his faith. He did, however, very much need a confessor to absolve his sins. He said that he was very aware of his faults, but didn't let them bother him. He would confess them to God regularly, but not beg Him for forgiveness. After confession, he would peacefully continue with his usual routine of love and adoration.

When he felt troubled, Brother Lawrence would not consult his peers. Knowing through his deep faith that God was with him, he was content with simply devoting all his actions to God – doing them with a desire to please Him, come what may.

He advised me that useless thoughts are dangerous, and the precursor to sin, and that as soon as we recognize that they are not useful in what we are doing, or for our salvation, we should reject them and return to prayer.

He said that in the beginning, he had often spent his appointed prayer time in rejecting unwanted thoughts wandering into his head, and then falling back into them. He had a hard time focusing during these times, failing even when using methods others successfully used. He did generally manage to meditate for a while, but he would eventually lose his focus, and go back to his usual wandering thoughts, and he couldn't describe how it happened.

Brother Lawrence stated that all exercises of bodily mortification, such as fasting and abstinence, are useless, unless they serve to bring you closer to God by love. He had thought about this often, and found that the shortest way to go straight to God was by continuous acts of love, and doing everything for Him.

He advised that we should understand the difference between acts of understanding, and those of intent. The acts we commit based on the understanding of our minds are of little value, but the intentions of our hearts are everything. Our only purpose is to love and be delighted by God.

He said that, no matter what ways we choose to use to discipline ourselves, we cannot rid ourselves of a single sin if those methods are empty of God's love. We should fearlessly accept that all our sins have already been cleansed by the blood of Jesus Christ, and concern ourselves only with Him, with all our hearts. God appears to offer the most grace to the biggest sinners, showing us how great is His mercy.

Brother Lawrence said that neither the pain nor the pleasure experienced in the physical world could be compared to those he had experienced in the spiritual state. As a result, he wasn't concerned or afraid of anything; all he wanted was to not offend God.

He claimed had no concern for those times when he sinned, saying, "When I fail in my duty, I readily acknowledge it, saying 'I am accustomed to failure, and I will never do better if left on my own.' If I do not fail, I give thanks to God, knowing that the strength came from Him."

Third Conversation

Brother Lawrence told me that the foundation of his spiritual life had been his high esteem and faith in God, and that once he realized these feelings, he wanted only to faithfully reject every other thought, and perform all his actions only for the love of God. He said that if he caught himself having not thought of God for some time, he did not allow it to concern him, but spoke to God of his lack of attentiveness, and returned to Him with far greater trust in Him, knowing how terrible it had felt to forget about Him.

He said that the trust we put in God greatly honors Him, and brings down His grace upon us.

He said that it is impossible, not only for God to deceive us, but also that He would allow a soul to suffer for long, if that soul is dedicated to Him, and committed to enduring everything for the sake of God.

Brother Lawrence said that he had so often experienced the assistance of Divine Grace when he needed it, that he no longer thought about a task before the time came to complete it. When it was time to complete the task, he would look to God, and see, as if in a clear mirror, exactly what he needed to do. In recent times, this behavior had become a habit, and something he didn't have to think about doing, but he had initially used it intentionally.

When his worldly tasks prevented him from thinking about God for a short while, God would send Brother Lawrence a sense of Himself to remember Him by, and Brother Lawrence's soul would be consumed by that memory. He would suddenly feel so passionate, and so distant from the physical world, that he could barely contain his excitement.

He said that he felt closer to God when he was working on worldly tasks, than when he was practicing his devotion alone in silence.

Brother Lawrence said that he expected, at some point in the future, to experience some great pain, either mental or physical. He thought that the worst thing that could happen to him would be to lose the sense of God that had brought him joy for so long, but he was reassured by

God's goodness, believing that he would never be completely forsaken. He knew that God would give him the strength to endure whatever difficulty He allowed to happen to him, so Brother Lawrence feared nothing, and felt no need to consult with anyone about his spiritual concerns. Whenever he had tried to speak to people about this, he had always left feeling more confused, and since he knew he was willing to give his life for the love of God, he had no concern for danger.

He said that being completely resigned to God is a sure way to get to Heaven; a way in which we would always be able to see our own behavior clearly.

Brother Lawrence said that in the beginning of our spiritual lives, we should be dedicated to doing our expected duties, and denying ourselves worldly comforts, but that after that, indescribable pleasures will follow. When we experience difficult times, we need only turn to Jesus Christ, and beg His divine gifts, and everything will become easy.

He said that many people do not advance in their faith, because they get stuck on repeated penances and spiritual exercises, neglecting the love of God, which is all that matters. He said that this is obvious when watching their behavior, and that it is the reason why we see so few truly virtuous people.

He said that neither art nor science are required for one's spiritual journey, but only a heart absolutely committed to doing only God's work, and to loving only Him.

Fourth Conversation

Brother Lawrence spoke with me often, and very openly from his heart, about his way of going to God. Some of this I have already discussed.

He told me that it essentially boils down to a solid rejection of everything we know does not lead to God, and that through this, we will become accustomed to continual conversation with Him, in a way that is simple and free. We only need to understand that God is with us at all times, and to speak to Him throughout the day, to beg His help if we are unsure of His will. When it is clear what He wants us to do, we should offer those actions to Him, and give Him thanks when we have completed them.

He said that in this perpetual conversation with God, we should also be constantly praising, loving, and adoring Him for His infinite goodness and perfection.

Brother Lawrence said that we should not feel discouraged by our sins, but that we should pray for God's grace with absolute confidence, relying on the endless virtue of our Lord Jesus Christ. He said that God never fails to offer us His forgiveness each time we sin, and that he could see this clearly, and never forgot to hand his sins to God, except if his mind had wandered away from the sense of God's presence for a time, or if he had forgotten to ask for God's help.

He told me that if we have no other desire than to please God, He would always enlighten us when we were feeling doubtful.

He said that to make ourselves holy, we did not need to change all our actions, but rather give those actions to God – do for Him what we would otherwise do for ourselves. He was always sad to see people thinking that their actions were the final aim, becoming addicted to completing certain religious actions, but doing them imperfectly, because of their human or selfish feelings.

Brother Lawrence said that the best way he had found of going to God was by going about our everyday tasks without aiming to please people, and by doing everything, as much as possible, for the love of God.

He said that it was a misconception to think that times of prayer should be separate from other times: he said that we are obliged to stay close to God through our actions when we are working, as much as we should while praying during dedicated times of prayer.

He told me that his praying was nothing more than a sense of the presence of God, and that while he prayed, his soul was completely unaware of anything except Divine love. He said that when his dedicated prayer times had passed, he felt no difference, because he continued in the same way, praising and blessing God with all his might, which allowed him to live his life in continual joy. He often hoped that God would give him some suffering, so that he could grow stronger through those lessons.

Brother Lawrence told me that we should, once and for all, put our whole trust in God, and surrender ourselves to Him completely, secure in the knowledge that He would never deceive us.

He said that we should not grow tired of doing little things for the love of God, as He doesn't pay attention to the size of the work, but only the love we have for Him while we do it. He said that we should not be surprised if we fail in the beginning, in our attempts to create religious habits. Rather, we should be pleasantly surprised when we find that those habits have been formed, that will cause us to naturally act the way we had hoped, without effort, and in a way that causes us great joy.

He told me that the whole substance of religion is faith, hope, and charity, and that by practicing these things, we become united with the will of God. Nothing else truly matters, except as a way to get to the point where we are embraced by faith and charity.

He said that all things are possible to those who believe, but even less difficult to those with hope. Those with love find things even easier than that, and people who work on the practice of all three virtues will find life easier than all others.

All we should ask ourselves to become in this life are the most perfect worshippers of God that we can possibly be, as we hope to continue to be throughout all eternity in Heaven.

Brother Lawrence said that when we enter into the spiritual life, we should examine ourselves closely, and think deeply about what we are. And then we should understand that we are inherently sinful, and worthy of disapproval, and that we don't even deserve to be called

Christians. We are subject to all sorts of misery and accidents, which cause us emotional and health issues, which cause regular changes in our physical bodies and mental personalities. God chooses to humble us through suffering and pain, both mental and physical. Knowing this, we should not be surprised when troubles, temptations, and arguments come to us from our fellow humans. Rather, we should accept these difficulties, and bear them for as long as God wants us to, seeing them as highly advantageous to our growth, and our journey to God.

The more a soul tries to become perfect, the more Divine grace it will need.

When asked by someone from his own order, whom he was obliged to answer, how he had obtained such a constant sense of God, Brother Lawrence told him that since he had first arrived at the monastery, he had thought of God as the purpose of all his thoughts and desires; that God was the goal to which they aspired, and the point at which they would all be fulfilled.

He told his superior that in the beginning of his time at the monastery, he had spent his dedicated private prayer hours thinking of God. He aimed to deeply convince his mind and heart of the Divine existence of God, through devout thinking and complete submission to his faith, rather than by meditating, or thinking about the methods of other religious scholars. He said that in this simple and sure way, he had created a lasting habit of living with the sense of God and His love. He decided at that time to do everything in his power to live in a continual sense of God's presence, and as far as possible, never to forget Him again, even for a moment.

He said that when he had spent his prayer time filling his mind with great thoughts of that infinite Being, he would go to his work in the kitchen (he was a cook for the monastery at that time), think first about the things that needed to be done there, and when and how each thing should be done, and then he would spend all his time between each job, and after his work, in prayer.

He said that when he started his work, he would say to God, with the trust of a son for his Father, "Oh, my God, since You are with me, and I must now, in order to be obedient to Your command, turn my mind to these outward tasks, I beg You to grant me the grace to continue in Your presence. I ask that You will help me to do the best I can at my job, and that You will accept all my hard work, as well as my affection."

As he went on with his work through the day, he would speak regularly to his Maker in a familiar way, asking for His grace, and offering up to Him all his actions.

When he finished work, he would look back over the day, and examine how he had carried out his duties. If he felt he had done well, he would give thanks to God, but if he felt he had not done his best, he would ask God's forgiveness. He would not feel discouraged if he had not done the best he could, but rather, he would set his mind right again, and go right back to his focus on the presence of God, as if he had never strayed from it. "And so," he said, "by rising after my falls, and by constantly restarting my acts of faith and love, I bring myself to a state in which it would be as difficult for me not to think of God, as it was to first become used to doing it all the time."

Because Brother Lawrence had found so much advantage in living in the presence of God, it was natural for him to strongly recommend it to others, but his actions and way of life set a far better example to those around him than anything he could say to convince them. Even his face was convincing, as it showed such a sweet and calm devotion to God, that nobody could ignore the effect it had on them. People often noticed that even when he was very busy while working in the kitchen, he always maintained his thoughts of God, and his heavenly-mindedness. He was never too rushed, and never lazy, but did each thing as it needed to be done, with a steady nature and calmness of spirit. As he said, "the time of work does not differ, for me, from the time of prayer. And in the noise and clatter of the kitchen, while several people are shouting for different things at once, I am as close to God, and in as much peace, as if I were kneeling in silence at the blessed sacrament."

LETTERS

Introduction: Brother Lawrence's letters are the very heart and soul of what is titled, 'The Practice of the Presence of God'. All of these letters were written during the last ten years of his life. Many of them were to long-time friends; a Carmelite sister, and a sister at a nearby convent. One or both of these friends were from his native village, perhaps relatives.

The first letter was probably written to the prioress of one of these convents. The second letter was written to Brother Lawrence's own spiritual adviser. Note that the fourth letter is written in the third person, and is a description of Brother Lawrence's own experiences.

First Letter

Since you so sincerely want me to tell you about the method I used to arrive at that habitual sense of God's presence, which our merciful Lord has graciously given into my care, I must tell you that I am very reluctant to give in to your insistence. I do it now, only on condition that you show my letter to nobody. If I thought that you would show it to anyone, no matter how much I want you to succeed, I would not be willing to do this. What I can tell you is the following:

I read many books, and found in them many ways of going to God, and many different spiritual practices, but I felt that they would confuse me, rather than help me get to where I wanted to be, which was only to belong completely to God. This made me decide to give my all for the All. So after giving myself entirely to God, that he might take away my sins, for the love of Him, I let go of everything that was not Him, and I started to live as though there were nobody in the world but me and Him. Sometimes, in God's presence, I felt like a poor criminal at the feet of a judge; at other times I felt like He was both my Father and my God. I worshipped Him as often as I could, keeping my mind linked to His holy presence, and any time I felt my thoughts wandering from Him, I called them back. I struggled with this exercise, but I continued with it, despite all the difficulties that occurred, without worrying or stressing about it when my mind wandered involuntarily. I made this my job, as much throughout the day as during my dedicated prayer times, because, at all times, every hour, every minute, even when I was very busy with work, I drove away from my mind everything that could interrupt my thoughts of God.

This has been my common practice ever since I became religious, and although I have done it very imperfectly, I have always found great advantage in it. These advantages, I am well aware, are a result of the virtue of the mercy and goodness of God, because we can do nothing without Him, and I even less than others. But when we are faithful at keeping ourselves in His holy presence, and placing Him always ahead of ourselves, not only does this prevent us from offending Him, and doing anything that might displease Him, on purpose, at least, but it also creates in us a holy freedom, and if I may be so bold, a familiarity with God which allows us to successfully ask for His grace when we need it. Basically, by repeating these acts as regularly as possible, we create a solid habit, and the presence of God becomes natural to us. Please join with me in thanking God for His great goodness towards me, for which my admiration can never be enough, and for the many favors He has done for such a miserable sinner as me. May all things praise Him. Amen.

Second Letter

To the Reverend,

I have not found my way to this life through books, and although I accept that, I would like to hear your thoughts on it for confirmation.

In a conversation a few days ago with a pious person, I was told that the spiritual life is a life of grace. It begins with a fear of punishment, and is then increased by the hope of eternal life, and eventually consummated by pure love. He told me that each of these states has its own stages though which we must travel, to arrive eventually at that blessed consummation.

I have not followed all these methods. In fact, I don't know why, but I found them discouraging to me. This is why, when I entered the spiritual life, I decided to give myself up to God, as that was all I could give Him in exchange for His love. And for His love, I renounced everything else.

For the first year, during my times of devotion, I generally kept myself busy with thoughts of death, judgement, Heaven, Hell, and my sins. This went on for a number of years longer, and I would carefully focus my mind for the rest of the day, even during busy work hours, on the presence of God, who I always thought of as being with me; often in me.

Eventually, without realizing it, I started doing the same thing during my dedicated prayer times, which made me feel very happy, and much better about myself. Doing this work gave me such a high esteem for God, that faith alone was enough to satisfy me.

This was how the spiritual life began for me, but I must tell you that for the first ten years, I suffered a lot. The fear that I was not devoted to God as much as I wanted to be, constant thoughts of my past sins, and the big and undeserved favors that God did for me, were the subject and source of my suffering. During this time, I fell often from God, but always raised myself quickly again. Sometimes I felt like all creation, logic, and even God Himself were against me, and all I had was my faith. I sometimes worried that to assume that such favors had been granted me by God was presumptuous; how could I have reached a point so easily, that others struggled to reach. At other times I felt it was an intentional delusion on my part, and that there was no hope of salvation for me.

Just when I had started to believe that I would live my whole life in these troubles, which did not cause me to trust God less, but rather served to increase my faith, I found myself abruptly changed, and my troubled soul felt suddenly peaceful, as if it had found its place in the world.

Ever since then, I live my life before God, simply, with faith, humility and love, and I diligently work to do and think nothing that would displease Him. I hope that when I have done my part, He will do with me what He wants.

As for my current way of life, I cannot explain it. I have no pain or suffering about my current state, because I have no will of my own, only God's will, which I aim to carry out in every action. I am so resigned to God's will that I would not do the smallest action if He did not wish it, or for any other reason than to show my love for Him.

I have stopped all forms of dedicated devotion and prayer times, aside from those that I must take part in in my position. And I make it my only job to live in His holy presence, which I keep myself mindful of by simple attention and a general fondness for God. I call this the presence of God, but it may be better described as a habitual, silent, and secret conversation of the soul with God, which often causes me such great joy and ecstasy inwardly, and sometimes outwardly, that I have to force myself to calm them and hide them from others.

Basically, I am absolutely certain, beyond a doubt, that my soul has been with God for the last thirty years. I am leaving out many things so that I don't become boring to you, but I think it is the right thing to explain to you how I find myself before God, whom I see as my King.

I think of myself as the most worthless of men, corrupt and pestilent, having committed all sorts of crimes against my King. Feeling a sensible regret, I confess all my wickedness to Him; I ask His forgiveness, I give myself to Him completely, that He may do with me what He pleases. The King, full of mercy and goodness, instead of reprimanding me, embraces me with love, makes me eat at His table, serves me with His own hands, gives me the key to His treasures. He talks happily to me, constantly, showing me in thousands of ways, He treats me as His favorite. This is how I sometimes consider myself to be in His holy presence.

My most useful method is this simple attention, as well as such a general passionate regard for God, that I often find myself attached to Him, with more sweetness and joy than a baby to its mother's breast. If I dare use the expression, I would call this state 'the bosom of God', because of the indescribable sweetness which I taste and experience in that state.

If my thoughts sometimes wander away from this state, because of necessity or my own humanness, I am quickly called back by inward emotions so charming and delicious that I am ashamed to mention them. I am asking for your reverence to reflect rather on my great wretchedness, of which you are fully aware, than upon the great favors which God has granted me, despite my unworthiness and ungratefulness.

As for my dedicated hours of prayer, they are only a continuation of the same practices. Sometimes I think of myself as a piece of stone, standing in front of a carver, ready to be made into a statue. Presenting myself to God in this way, I want Him to form His perfect image in my soul, and make me like Him.

At other times, when I sit at prayer, I feel my whole soul lift up of its own accord, with no effort from me, and suspend, as if it is firmly settled in God, in its intended place of peace.

I know that some feel this state is one of inactivity, delusion, and self-love. I admit that it is a holy inactivity, and would be a happy self-love if the soul could love itself in that state. In effect, while the soul is in this state, it cannot be disturbed by the acts it was previously accustomed to, and which previously supported it, but would now rather hinder than help it.

However, I cannot bear to think of this state as a delusion, because the soul that enjoys God in this way wants nothing but Him. If this is a delusion I am enjoying, it is then God's place to fix it. Let Him do as He wants with me – I want only Him, and to be completely devoted to Him. Please do send me your opinion on this matter, as I always hold your opinion in high regard, because I have high esteem for your reverence. I am yours in our Lord.

Third Letter

We have a God who is infinitely gracious, and knows all our needs. I always thought that He would reduce you to extremity. He will come in His own time, and when you least expect it. Put your hope in Him, more than ever, and thank Him with me for the favors He does for you, and especially for the strength and patience He gives you to deal with your condition. It is an obvious sign of how much He cares for you. Allow that to comfort you, and be thankful for everything.

I also admire the strength and bravery of Mr. [Name Unknown]. God has given him a good personality, and a good nature, but he still has in him a bit of worldliness and immaturity. I hope that the injury God has sent him will be a good influence on him, and cause him to look more closely at himself. It is an incident which will hopefully cause him to put all of his trust in God, who is always with him. Let him think of God as often as he can, especially in the greatest dangers. Just a little act of handing the heart to God is enough. A small remembrance of Him, one act of inward worship, even while marching with sword in hand, are prayers, which no matter how short, are still very acceptable to God. Rather than taking away a soldier's courage when in danger, they only help to strengthen it.

So let him think of God as much as he can. Let him slowly become used to doing this small, but holy exercise. No one will notice it, and nothing could be easier than to often repeat these little internal prayers of adoration throughout the day. Recommend to him, please, that he should think of God as much as he can, as I have described above. It is a good and necessary practice for a soldier, who is exposed daily to the dangers of life. I hope that God will assist him and all the family, to whom I offer my service, being theirs and yours.

Fourth Letter

I have taken this opportunity to tell you about the thoughts of a member of the monastery, regarding the wonderful effects and continual help he receives from the presence of God. Let you and me both profit from them. *(Brother Lawrence is talking about himself in the third person in this letter.)*

You must know that his continual purpose, for about the past 40 years that he has spent in religion, has been to always be with God, and to do, say, and think nothing which could displease Him. He does this with no other motive than to love God, and because He deserves infinitely more than that.

He is now so accustomed to that Divine Presence, that he receives from it continual support on all occasions. For about 30 years, his soul has been filled with such great and continual joys, that he is forced to try and moderate them, and to prevent himself from showing them outwardly, as many around him may not understand.

If he sometimes finds himself away from that Divine Presence for a bit too long, God will make Himself felt in his soul, to call him back, which often happens when he is most caught up in his worldly business. He answers with strong loyalty to these inward callings, either by lifting his heart up to God, or by thinking humbly and fondly of Him, or by using whatever words of love build up in him on these occasions. For example, he may say, "My God, here I am, devoted to You. Lord, make me according to Your heart". And then it seems to him, as he feels the effects, that this God of love, satisfied with such few words, calms again, and rests in the center of his soul. The experience of these things gives him such an assurance that God is always in the bottom of his soul, that it makes him completely unable to doubt it under any circumstances.

You can imagine what contentment and satisfaction he enjoys, while always finding in himself such a great treasure. He is no longer anxiously searching for it, but has it open in front of him, and can take what he needs from it.

He often complains that we are blind, and cries that we should be pitied for being happy with so little. He says that God has infinite treasure to give, yet we offer only a little routine devotion, which passes in a moment. Blind as we are, we hinder God, and stop the flow of His graces. But when He finds a soul which is full of a lively faith, He pours His graces and favors into it plentifully. There they will flow like a river which has been forcibly stopped, and then found a new passage, spreading itself impulsively and excessively.

Yes, we often stop this river by placing too little value upon it. But let us stop it no more; let us look inside ourselves and break down the bank which hinders it. Let us make room for grace, and let us make up for lost time, because we may only have a little left. Death follows us closely, so let us be well prepared for it. We only die once, and we cannot correct our mistakes afterwards.

I say again, let us look inside ourselves. Time moves on, and there is no time to waste: our souls are at stake. I believe you have taken the right measures, and will not be surprised. I commend you for it; it is the only necessary thing. But we must always work at it, because if we are not advancing in the spiritual life, we are going backwards. But those who have the gale of the Holy Spirit move forward, even in their sleep. If the ship of the soul is still battered with winds and storms, let us wake the Lord who rests in it, and He will quickly calm the sea.

I have taken the liberty to share these good thoughts with you, that you may compare them to your own. It will help to once again kindle them to burning, if they are (God forbid) unfortunately cooled, despite never being small to begin with. So let us both recall our early passions. Let us profit by the example and the thoughts of this Brother, who is little known by the world, but is known by God, and well cared for by Him. I will pray for you; please pray right away for me, who am, in our Lord, yours.

I received today two books and a letter from Sister [Name Unknown], who is preparing to make her Vows, and wishes the prayers of your holy society, and yours in particular. I can see that she puts her faith in them, please do not disappoint her. Beg of God that she may make her sacrifice in the view of His love alone, and with a strong resolve to be completely devoted to Him. I will send you one of these books, which discuss the presence of God; a subject which I believe contains the whole spiritual life. It seems to me that whoever practices the presence of God will soon become spiritually devout.

I know that to practice it correctly, one's heart must be empty of all other things, because God will possess the heart alone, and He cannot possess it alone without emptying it of all besides Himself. And He cannot act in the heart, and do in it what He pleases, unless it is left empty for Him.

There doesn't exist in the world a life more sweet and delightful than that of a continual conversation with God. Only those who practice and experience it can understand it, but I do not advise you to do it for that reason. It is not pleasure that we should be seeking from this exercise. We should be doing it from a place of love, and because God wants us.

If I were a preacher, I would preach the practice of the presence of God above all things, and if I were a spiritual adviser, I would advise all the world to do it. That is how important and easy I believe it to be.

If only we knew the need we have for the grace and assistance of God, we would never lose sight of Him, not for a moment. Believe me, you should immediately make a strong, holy decision to never again intentionally forget Him, and to spend the rest of your life in His sacred presence, deprived, for the love of Him, of all comforts, should He wish it.

Set about this work vigorously, and if you do it as you should, rest assured that you will soon feel the effects of it. I will help you with my prayers, as insignificant as they are. I offer my sincere regards to you, and those of your holy society, being theirs, and more particularly yours.

Sixth Letter

To the same,

I have received from Mrs. [Name Unknown] the things which you gave her for me. I wonder why you have not given me your thoughts about the little book I sent to you, which you must have received. You should enthusiastically start practicing it in your old age – it is better late than never.

I cannot imagine how religious people can feel satisfied in their lives without the practice of the presence of God. For my part, I live with Him in the depths of my soul as much as I can, and while I am with Him, I fear nothing. But the smallest turning away from Him is intolerable.

This exercise does not much exhaust the body, but it is right to deprive it sometimes, no, often, of many little pleasures which are innocent and lawful, because God will not allow a soul that wants to be completely devoted to

Him to take other enjoyment, and that is more than reasonable.

I am not saying that we must therefore put extremely strict restrictions on ourselves. No, we must serve God in holy freedom – we must do our jobs faithfully, without stress or unhappiness, bringing our minds back to God gently and calmly, whenever we find them wandering away from Him.

However, it is necessary to put our whole trust in God, laying aside all other concerns, and even some particular forms of devotion. Even though these forms of devotion are very good in themselves, we often engage in them unreasonably, because they are a means of reaching the end. When, by the practice of the presence of God, we are with Him who is our end, it is useless to return to the means. But we may continue in our love of Him, and persevere through His holy presence. We can do this by an act of praise, adoration or desire, or we can do it by an act of submission or thanksgiving, or in any other ways our spirit can invent.

Do not be discouraged by the dislike you may find for this practice in the beginning – you must be strict with yourself. In the beginning, it may feel like a waste of time, but you must go on, and decide to push through with it until death, no matter the difficulties that may arise. I ask for the prayers of your holy society, and yours in particular. I am, in our Lord, yours.

Seventh Letter

I feel very sorry for you. It will be of great help if you can leave the care of your affairs to [Name Unknown], and spend the remainder of your life only in worshipping God. He doesn't ask much of us: just a little remembrance of Him from time to time, a little adoration, some prayers for His grace, some prayers to tell Him of your suffering, some prayers to give Him thanks for His favors, which He still gives you in the midst of your troubles, and to comfort yourself with Him as often as you can. Lift up your heart to Him, sometimes even at your mealtimes, and when you are with other people – the smallest remembrance will always be enough for Him. You do not need to pray out loud; He is closer to us than we think.

It is not necessary for us to always be at Church, to be with God: we can make a private chapel in our hearts which we can withdraw to, sometimes, to speak to Him in humbleness, humility, and love. Everyone is capable of such familiar conversation with God, some more, some less – He knows what we can do, so let us begin. Maybe He only expects one strong commitment from us. Have courage. We don't have long to live. You are nearly 64, and I am almost 80. Let us live and die with God. Sufferings will be sweet and pleasant to us while we are with Him, but the greatest pleasures would be a cruel punishment to us without Him. May He be praised for everything. Amen.

Start training yourself slowly to worship Him in this way; to beg His grace, to offer Him your heart every now and then while you are working, even every moment, if you can. Do not always confine yourself to strict rules or particular forms of devotion, but live with general confidence in God, with love and humility. You may assure [Name Unknown] of my insignificant prayers, and that I am their servant, and particularly yours, in our Lord.

Eighth Letter

(About wandering thoughts during prayer).

This is nothing new to me – you are not the only one who struggles with wandering thoughts. Our minds are extremely rambling, but because our will is the mistress of all our abilities, she must bring our stray thoughts back, and carry them to God as their final destination.

When the mind, not being properly controlled during our early times of devotion, has learned bad habits of wandering and indulgence, they can be difficult to overcome, and make us think, even against our wills, about things of the earth.

I believe that one cure for this is to confess our faults, and to humble ourselves before God. I do not advise you to use too many words in prayer, because during long speeches is often the time that our minds wander. When you are before God in prayer, behave like a mute or paralytic beggar at a rich man's gate. Let it be your job to keep your mind in the presence of the Lord. If it sometimes wanders and withdraws itself from Him, do not be unhappy about it – stress and unhappiness will distract the mind further, rather than bringing it back to God. Use your will to bring it back peacefully. If you keep trying in this way, God will take pity on you.

One way to bring the mind back easily when you are in prayer, and to keep it there peacefully, is to not let it wander too far during other times. You should keep it strictly in the presence of God, and if you become accustomed to thinking of Him often, you will find it easy to keep your mind calm during the time of prayer, or at least to call it back from its wanderings.

I have told you already, many times, in my previous letters, of the advantages we can gain from this practice of the presence of God. Let us get started on it seriously, and pray for each other.

Yours.

Ninth Letter

The enclosed letter is an answer to that which I received from [Name Unknown], please deliver it to her. It seems to me that she has good intentions, but she wants to move faster than grace. We cannot become holy quickly. I recommend her to you: we should help each other with our advice, and even more by our good examples. I'd like to hear about her every now and then, and whether she is enthusiastic and obedient.

So let us often remember that our only job in this life is to please God, and that everything else is nothing but foolishness and vanity. You and I have lived about 40 years in the monastic life. Have we spent them loving and serving God, who by His mercy has called us to this life, and for that reason? I am filled with shame and confusion when I think about the great favors that God has done, and constantly continues to do for me, and on the other hand, how badly I have used them, and how little I have advanced towards perfection.

Since God is merciful, and has granted us a little more time, let us sincerely start: let's make up for the lost time, and pledge ourselves once again to our God of mercy, who is always ready to receive us affectionately. For the love of God, let us completely reject everything that is not Him; He deserves so much more. Let us think of Him at all times, and let us put our trust in Him. I have no doubt that we will soon feel the effects of it when we receive His abundant grace, with which we can do anything, and without which all we can do is sin.

We cannot escape the many dangers in life without the real and constant help of God, so let us pray to Him for it constantly. How can we pray to Him without being with Him? How can we be with Him unless we are thinking of Him often? And how can we think of Him often, unless we form a holy habit of doing it? You will tell me that I am always saying the same thing. It is true, because this is the best, and easiest method I know, and since I don't use any others, I advise everyone to do it like this. We must know before we can love. To know God, we must think of Him often, and when we learn to love God, we will think of Him often, because our hearts will be with our treasure. This is an opinion that strongly deserves your consideration.

I am yours.

Tenth Letter

I have had a hard time convincing myself to write to Mr. [Name Unknown], and I am doing it now, only because you and Madam [Name Unknown] want me to. Please write his address and send it to Him. I am very pleased with the trust you have in God, and I hope that He will continue to increase it in you. We can never have too much trust in such a good and faithful Friend, who will never fail us in this world or the next.

If Mr. [Name Unknown] makes the most of his loss, and puts all his trust in God, He will soon provide him with another friend; one who is more powerful, and more motivated to serve him. God does with our hearts as He pleases. Perhaps Mr. [Name Unknown] was too attached to the one he has lost. We should love our friends, but it shouldn't encroach on the love we owe to God, which must be our primary love.

Please remember my advice to you, which is to think of God often, day and night, during your work, and even during your free time. He is always near you and with you; do not leave Him alone. You would think it rude to leave a friend alone if he had come to visit you, so why must God be neglected? Do not forget Him, but think about Him often, adore Him continually, live and die with Him. This is the glorious job of a Christian. To put it simply, this is our profession; if we do not know it, we must learn it. I will try to help you with my prayers, and am, in our Lord, yours.

Eleventh Letter

I do not pray that your pains will be taken away, but I earnestly ask God to give you the strength and patience to bear them as long as He pleases. Take comfort in Him who gives you this pain. He will take it away when He thinks it right. Happy are those who suffer with Him: become accustomed to suffering, and look to God for the strength to endure as much as He judges to be necessary for you, and for as long as He wants. Worldly men do not understand these truths, and it's not surprising, since they suffer as worldly men, not as Christians. They think that illness is a natural problem, rather than a gift from God, and seeing it that way, they find only grief and distress in it. But those who consider sickness as coming from the hand of God, as the effect of His mercy, and His means towards their salvation, often find it comforting and consoling.

I wish you could convince yourself that God is often, in some ways, closer to us, and more actively with us, in sickness than in health. Do not rely upon any doctor, because I believe God keeps your cure to Himself. So put all your trust in Him, and you will soon feel the effects of it when you start to recover. We often prevent our own recovery by putting more trust in science than in God.

Whatever medications you use can only work as much as God allows. When pains come from God, only He can cure them. He often sends diseases of the body to cure those of the soul. Take comfort in the care of the supreme Doctor of both the body and the soul.

Be satisfied with the condition God has given you. However happy you think I am, I envy you. Pain and suffering would be paradise to me while I suffer with my God, and the greatest pleasures would be Hell to me if I could enjoy them without Him. My greatest comfort would be to suffer through something for His sake.

I must shortly go to God. What comforts me in this life is that I now see God by faith, and I see Him in a way that might make me say, sometimes, "I no longer believe, but now I see". I feel what faith teaches us, and with that knowledge, and that practice of faith, I will live and die with Him.

Go always with God; it is the only comfort and support for your illness. I will beg Him to be with you. I offer you my service. Yours.

Twelfth Letter

If we were all used to the exercise of the presence of God, all physical illnesses would be significantly relieved by it. God often allows us to suffer a bit, to purify our souls, and help us to live our lives with Him.

Take courage, and offer up your pains to God continuously. Pray to Him for the strength to endure them. Most importantly, create a habit of keeping yourself busy with God, and forget Him as little as you can. Adore Him while you are ill, offer yourself to Him every now and then, and in the worst of your suffering, beg Him humbly and affectionately, as a child would beg his father, to make you shapeable to His holy will. I will try to assist you with my meager prayers.

God has many ways of bringing us to Himself. He sometimes hides Himself from us, but faith must be our support, and never fail us in our times of need. It must be the basis of our confidence, which must be entirely in God.

I don't know how God will deal with me. I am always happy. All the world suffers, but I, who deserve the severest discipline, feel such continual and great joys that I can barely contain them.

I would willingly ask God for a part of your suffering, except that I know my weakness. It is so great that if God left me alone for one moment, I would be the most worthless man alive. And yet, I don't know how He could leave me alone, because faith gives me the strongest belief possible, that God never forsakes us unless we forsake Him first. Let us be afraid to leave Him. Let us always be with Him. Let us live and die in His presence. Please pray for me, as I will for you.

I am yours.

Thirteenth Letter

To the Same,

It hurts me to see you suffer for so long. What relieves
that pain, and sweetens the feelings I have for your grief,
is that they are proof of God's love for you. If you see
them that way, you will be able to handle them more
easily. In your case, I believe that you should stop using
human remedies, and give yourself completely to the
wisdom of God. Perhaps all He is waiting for is that
submission, and a perfect trust in Him, to cure you.
Since, despite all the medical care you have received,
science has until now proved unsuccessful, and your
illness continues to get worse, you would not be testing
God if you were to hand yourself over to His hands, and
expect everything from Him.

I told you in my last letter that God sometimes allows
physical illnesses to cure the diseases of the soul. So take
courage, and turn this necessary situation into a virtue.

Do not ask God to deliver you from your pain, but rather for the strength to bear with determination, for the love of Him, all that He wants, for as long as He wants.

These kinds of prayers are naturally a bit difficult for us, but they are very acceptable to God, and enjoyable to those who love Him. Love sweetens pain, and when you love God, you will suffer for His sake with joy and courage. I beg you to do this: take comfort in Him who is the only doctor of all our diseases. God is the Father of the diseased, and is always ready to help us. He loves us so much more than we can imagine. So love Him, and do not look for comfort elsewhere. I hope you will soon receive it. Goodbye. I will help you with my prayers, meager as they are, and will always be, in our Lord, yours.

Fourteenth Letter

To the Same,

I give thanks to our Lord for having relieved you a bit, as you wanted. I have often been close to death, and I've never been so content as I was then. Because of this, I did not pray for any relief, but I prayed for the strength to suffer with courage, humility, and love. Oh, how sweet it is to suffer with God! However big the sufferings may be, receive them with love. It is paradise to suffer and be with Him, and if we want to enjoy the peace of paradise in this life, we must create the habit of familiar, humble, and affectionate conversation with Him. We must stop our spirits from wandering away from Him at all times. We must make our hearts into spiritual temples, in which we can adore Him continuously. We must always watch over ourselves, and prevent ourselves from doing, saying, or thinking anything that may displease Him. When our minds are kept busy with God in this way, suffering will become soothing and comfortable.

I know that it is very difficult to arrive at this state in the beginning, because we have to act purely from faith. But although it is difficult, we also know that we can do all things with the grace of God, which He never refuses to those who ask for it sincerely. Knock, and keep knocking, and I guarantee that He will open to you when the time is right, and give you all that He has held back during many years. Goodbye! Pray to Him for me, as I pray to Him for you. I hope to see Him soon.

I am yours.

Fifteenth Letter

To the Same,

God knows best what we need, and everything He does is for our good. If we knew how much He loves us we would always be willing to receive, equally and with indifference, from Him, the sweet and the bitter. Anything coming from Him would please us. The worst difficulties never appear unbearable, unless we see them in the wrong light. When we see them as granted by the hand of God, when we know that it is our loving Father who humiliates and grieves us, our sufferings will lose their bitterness, and even become a matter of comfort.

Let all our occupation be to know God. The more we know Him, the more we want to know Him. As knowledge is the measure of love, the deeper and more extensively we know Him, the more we can love Him. And if our love for God is great, we will love Him equally in pain and in pleasure.

Let us not be content with loving God just for the favors, no matter how high, which He has done, or will do for us. Such favors, though very great, cannot bring us as near to Him as faith does, with one simple act. Let us look for Him often in our faith. He is within us, so do not look for Him elsewhere. If we love Him alone, would it not be rude, and should we not be blamed, if we allow ourselves to engage in trivialities which may displease and offend Him. We should fear that these trivialities will one day cost us dearly.

Let us start being devoted to Him in all seriousness. Let us cast out of our hearts, everything else. He wants to possess them alone. Beg Him for this favor. If we do what we can for our part, we will soon see the change in ourselves that we have been hoping for. I cannot thank Him enough for the relief He has given you. I hope He is merciful enough to let me see Him within a few days. Let us pray for one another.

I am, in our Lord, yours.

(Brother Lawrence died peacefully, shortly after writing this letter.)

SPIRITUAL MAXIMS

1. We should be considerate of God in everything we do and say. Our goal should be to become perfect in our adoration of Him throughout this earthly life in preparation for all eternity. We must make a firm resolution to overcome, with God's grace, all the difficulties encountered in a spiritual life.

2. From the very beginning of our Christian walk, we should remember who we are and that we are unworthy of the name of Christian, except for what Christ has done for us. In cleansing us from all our impurities, God desires to humble us and allow us to go through a number of trials or difficulties.

3. We must believe with certainty that it is both pleasing to God and good for us to sacrifice ourselves for Him. Without this complete

submission of our hearts and minds to His will, He cannot work in us to make us perfect.

4. The more we aspire to be perfect, the more dependent we are on the grace of God. We begin to need His help with every little thing and at every moment, because without it we can do nothing. The world, the flesh, and the devil wage a fierce and continuous war on our souls. If we weren't capable of humbly depending on God for assistance, our souls would be dragged down. Although this total dependence may sometimes go against our human nature, God takes great pleasure in it. That should bring us rest

Practice Necessary to Acquire the Spiritual Life

1. The most holy and necessary practice in our spiritual life is the presence of God. That means finding constant pleasure in His divine company, speaking humbly and lovingly with Him in all seasons, at every moment, without limiting the conversation in any way. This is especially important in times of temptation, sorrow, separation from God, and even in times of unfaithfulness and sin.

2. We must try to converse with God in little ways while we do our work; not in memorized prayer, not trying to recite previously formed thoughts. Rather, we should purely and simply reveal our hearts as the words come to us.

3. We must do everything with great care, avoiding impetuous actions, which are evidence of a disordered spirit. God wishes us to work gently,

calmly, and lovingly with Him, asking Him to accept our work. By this continual attention to God, we will "resist the devil and cause him to flee" (James 4:7).

4. Whatever we do, even if we are reading the Word or praying, we should stop for a few minutes — as often as possible — to praise God from the depths of our hearts, to enjoy Him there in secret. Since you believe that God is always with you, no matter what you may be doing, why shouldn't you stop for awhile to adore Him, to praise Him, to petition Him, to offer Him your heart, and to thank Him? What could please God more than for us to leave the cares of the world temporarily in order to worship Him in our spirits? These momentary retreats serve to free us from our selfishness, which can only exist in the world. In short, we cannot show God our loyalty to Him more than by renouncing our worldly selves as much as a thousand times a day to enjoy even a single moment with Him.

This doesn't mean you must leave the duties of the world forever; that would be impossible. Let prudence be your guide. But I do believe that it is a common mistake of spirit-filled persons not to leave the cares of the world from time to time to praise God in their spirits and to rest in the peace of His divine presence for a few moments.

5. Our adoration of God should be done in faith, believing that He really lives in our hearts, and that He must be loved and served in spirit and in truth. Believe that He is the most independent One, upon Whom all of us depend, and that He is aware of everything that happens to us. The Lord's perfections are truly beyond measure. By His infinite excellence and His sovereign place as both Creator and Savior, He has the right to possess us and all that exists in both heaven and earth. It should be His good pleasure to do with each of us whatever He chooses through all time and eternity. Because of all He is to us, we owe Him our thoughts, words and actions. Let us earnestly endeavor to do this.

6. We must carefully examine ourselves to see which virtues we are in most need of, and which we find the hardest to acquire. We should also take note of the sins that we most frequently fall into and what occasions often contribute to that fall. It is

in our times of struggle with these areas that we can go before God with entire confidence and remain firm in the presence of His divine Majesty. In humble adoration, we must confess to Him our sins and weaknesses, lovingly asking for the help of His grace in our time of need. In this way, we will find that we can partake of all the virtues found in Him, even though we do not possess one of our own.

How To Adore God in Spirit and In Truth

There are three points to consider here:

First, to adore God in Spirit and in truth means to adore Him as we should. Because God is a Spirit, He must be adored in spirit. That is to say, we must worship Him with a humble, sincere love that comes from the depth and center of our soul. Only God can see this adoration, which we must repeat until it becomes part of our nature, as if God were one with our soul and our soul were one with God. Practice will demonstrate this.

Secondly, to adore God in truth is to recognize Him for what He is, and ourselves for what we are. Adoring God in truth means that our heart actually sees God as infinitely perfect and worthy of our praise. What man, regardless of how little sense he may have, would not exert all his strength to show his respect and love of this great God?

Thirdly, to adore God in truth is to admit that our nature is just the opposite of His. Yet, He is willing to make us like Him, if we desire it. Who would be so rash as to neglect, even for a moment, the respect, the love, the service, and the continual adoration that we owe Him?

The Union of The Soul with God

The first way in which the soul is united with God is through salvation, solely by His grace.

This is followed by a period in which a saved soul comes to know God through a series of experiences, some of which bring it into closer union with Him and some take it further away. The soul learns which activities bring God's presence nearer. It remains in His presence by practicing those activities.

The most perfect union with God is the actual presence of God. Although this relationship with God is totally spiritual, it is quite dynamic, because the soul is not asleep, but powerfully excited. It is livelier than fire and brighter than the unclouded sun. Yet, it is at the same time tender and devout. It is not a simple expression of the heart, like saying, "Lord, I love You with all my heart," or other similar words. Rather, it is an inexpressible state of the soul — gentle, peaceful, respectful, humble, loving, and very simple — that urges it to love God, to adore Him, and to embrace Him with both tenderness and joy.

Everyone who is striving for divine union must realize that just because something is agreeable and delightful to the will does not mean that it will bring one closer to God. Sometimes it is helpful to disengage the sentiments of the will from the world, in order that it can focus entirely on God. For if the will is able in some manner to comprehend Him, it can be only by love. And that love, which has its end in God, will be hindered by the things of this world.

The presence of God is the concentration of the soul's attention on God, remembering that He is always present.

I know a person who for forty years has practiced the presence of God, to which he gives several other names. Sometimes he calls it a simple act — a clear and distinct knowledge of God, and sometimes he calls it a vague view or a general and loving look at God — a remembrance of Him. He also refers to it as attention to God, silent communion with God, confidence in God, or the life and the peace of the soul. To sum it up, this person has told me that all these manners of the presence of God are synonyms which signify the same thing, which have all become natural to him.

My friend says that by dwelling in the presence of God he has established such a sweet communion with the Lord that his spirit abides, without much effort, in the restful peace of God. In this rest, he is filled with a faith that equips him to handle anything that comes to him.

The Presence of God The presence of God is the concentration of the soul's attention on God, remembering that He is always present. I know a person who for forty years has practiced the presence of God, to which he gives several other names. Sometimes he calls it a simple act — a clear and distinct knowledge of God, and sometimes he calls it a vague view or a general and loving look at God — a remembrance of Him.

He also refers to it as attention to God, silent communion with God, confidence in God, or the life and the peace of the soul. To sum it up, this person has told me that all these manners of the presence of God are synonyms which signify the same thing, which have all become natural to him. My friend says that by dwelling in the presence of God he has established such a sweet communion with the Lord that his spirit abides, without much effort, in the restful peace of God. In this rest, he is filled with a faith that equips him to handle anything that comes to him.

The Means of Acquiring the Presence of God

1. The first means is a new life, received by salvation through the blood of Christ.

2. The second is faithfully practicing God's presence. This must always be done gently, humbly, and lovingly, without giving way to anxiety or problems.

3. The soul's eyes must be kept on God, particularly when something is being done in the outside world. Since much time and effort are needed to perfect this practice, one should not be discouraged by failure. Although the habit is difficult to form, it is a source of divine pleasure once it is learned. It is proper that the heart — which is the first to live and which dominates all the other parts of the body — should be the first and the last to love God. The heart is the beginning and the end of all our spiritual and

bodily actions and, generally speaking, of everything we do in our lives. It is, therefore, the heart whose attention we must carefully focus on God.

4. In the beginning of this practice, it would not be wrong to offer short phrases that are inspired by love, such as "Lord, I am all Yours," "God of love, I love You with all my heart," or "Lord, use me according to Your will." But remember to keep the mind from wandering or returning to the world. Hold your attention on God alone by exercising your will to remain in God's presence.

5. Although this exercise may be difficult at first to maintain, it has marvelous effects on the soul when it is faithfully practiced. It draws the graces of the Lord down in abundance and shows the soul how to see God's presence everywhere with a pure and loving vision, which is the holiest, firmest, easiest, and the most effective attitude for prayer.

1. The first blessing that the soul receives from the practice of the presence of God is that its faith is livelier and more active everywhere in our lives. This is particularly true in difficult times, since it obtains the grace we need to deal with temptation and to conduct ourselves in the world. The soul accustomed by this exercise to the practice of faith can actually see and feel God by simply entering His presence. It envokes Him easily and obtains what it needs. In so doing, the soul could be said to approach the Blessed, in that it can almost say, "I no longer believe, but I see and experience." Its faith becomes more and more penetrating as it advances through practice.

2. The practice of the presence of God strengthens us in hope. Our hope increases as our faith penetrates God's secrets through practice of our

holy exercise. The soul discovers in God a beauty infinitely surpassing not only that of bodies that we see on earth, but even that of the angels. Our hope increases and grows stronger, and the amount of good that it expects to enjoy, and that in some degree it tastes, reassures and sustains it.

3. This practice causes the will to rejoice at being set apart from the world, setting it aglow with the fire of holy love. This is because the soul is always with God, Who is a consuming fire, Who reduces into powder whatever is opposed to Him. The soul thus inflamed can no longer live except in the presence of its God. This presence produces a holy ardor, a sacred urgency, and a violent desire in the heart to see this God, Who is loved.

4. By practicing God's presence and continuously looking at Him, the soul familiarizes itself with Him to the extent that it passes almost its whole life in continual acts of love, praise, confidence, thanksgiving, offering, and petition. Sometimes all this may merge into one single act that does not end, because the soul is always in the ceaseless exercise of God's Divine presence.